How to be a GREAT Christian Leader

A practical workbook for leaders and those aspiring to be
Sample Chapter - Leader's Self-Assessment

MADGE OBASEKI

Copyright © 2019 by Madge Obaseki
All rights reserved. This book or any portion thereof
may not be reproduced or used in any manner whatsoever
without the express written permission of the publisher
except for the use of brief quotations in a book review.

Printed in the United States of America

First Printed, 2014. Second Edition, 2019

ISBN 978-1-9998397-7-2

Future Hope Legacy Publishing
International House, 776-778 Barking Road,
London, United Kingdom, E13 9PJ

TABLE OF CONTENTS

THE LEADER SELF-ASSESSMENT 1
    Why self-assess? 1
    How often do I need to self-assess? 2
    How your conduct as a leader influences outcome? 2
    What happens if the Self-Assessment shows that I have areas for improvement? 2
    What if I need extra support having completed the self-assessment? 2

LEADER SELF-ASSESSMENT INSTRUCTIONS 5
    How to use this self-assessment 5

INSTRUCTIONS FOR USE 6

COMMUNICATION SKILLS 7

TEAM BUILDING 8

ETHICS 10

LEADERSHIP 11

SUPPORT 14

THE LEADER SELF-ASSESSMENT

> A wise man once stated that leaders set the temperature. In other words, a leader influences what others do or follow. With that in mind, how often do leaders address their actions and their effect on the people they work with?
>
> If you have never assessed your leadership methods and their impact on others, I strongly recommend this exercise. Indeed, you will be at a disadvantage if you do not complete this process before accessing the full workbook How to be a GREAT Christian Leader.
>
> In short, the Leader's Self-Assessment will highlight your areas of strength and weaknesses.

Why self-assess?

One of my favourite verses in the bible is 2 Tim: 15. On Apostle Paul's advice, I believe we can always learn more and therefore grow as leaders. Thus, I devised this leader's self-assessment. The majority of leaders in the Church, ministry and the business world, have not had access to formal leadership training or development.

In my experience it seems to be common practice for some local churches to promote faithful workers to leadership positions without providing training and support. I also discovered that some seminaries, bible colleges, and some universities who offer theology and biblical studies, generally do not address Christian leadership as a discipline. I have observed as a result of a lack of training and development that some leaders unconsciously select a trial and error tactic with regrettable consequences.

I found completing the self-assessment tremendously helpful and I am confident you will too. The template helped me to make improvements to my leadership style and only took me just 20 minutes to complete.

How often do I need to self-assess?

If you have never done a self-assessment before, it might take you a little longer for the first time. You may find you are unable to complete it all at first possibly because you have not gained experience in some facets. As time goes on, you will be able to complete the self-assessment more fully, and it will become even more meaningful. The main idea is to monitor your areas for development/improvement, and continue to do so at regular intervals because like the seasons, your priorities can change.

How your conduct as a leader influences outcome?

The impact your conduct and style of leadership has on others be it staff, volunteers, and in business will influence your local church, ministry or organisation's ability to achieve mission and objectives. To ensure optimal results, a leader, should review their technique holistically, i.e. addressing all aspects. Once you carry out a self-assessment, you have an invaluable tool to help you address areas identified for improvement.

What happens if the Self-Assessment shows that I have areas for improvement?

Great! As I mentioned previously, the reason for including the self-assessment is to expose areas for development.

What if I need extra support having completed the self-assessment?

Once you have identified areas for development, you might feel you need support to address some of the issues raised. The bible tells us that in the wisdom book Proverbs 15: 22 that: *Without counsel, plans fail, but with many advisers, they succeed'* (ESV). I have three mentors for different areas of my business and ministry. They are a mix of individuals I either pay or are close contacts who I can consult when I need support.

I recommend you speak to someone who has more experience than you or operates in a broader field. They can often help you see things from a different angle. Ideally, the individual must be someone you can trust to keep your information confidential.

NOTES

LEADER SELF-ASSESSMENT INSTRUCTIONS

How to use this self-assessment

1. Complete this Self-Assessment before embarking on the rest of the full workbook, How to be a GREAT Christian Leader Workbook.
2. Use this Self-Assessment tool to test your strengths and weaknesses (some prefer the term 'areas for improvement')
3. Make adjustments as appropriate by seeking training or addressing areas for development.
4. Use this self-assessment on a regular basis to assess your progress.
5. Consider all your experiences including work, voluntary, business as well as your work in the local church, when answering each question
6. Even if you do not have individuals reporting to you yet, complete this self-assessment. This tool will help you formulate how you will respond when you start to lead others.

N.B.

IT IS IMPORTANT TO BE HONEST WITH YOURSELF WHILST

COMPLETING THIS IN ORDER TO GROW AND LEARN

INSTRUCTIONS FOR USE

Tick in the box which best corresponds for each question in line with your current experience

DATE COMPLETED: _____

COMMUNICATION SKILLS:	Almost Never	Rarely	Sometimes	Often	Almost Always	N/A
I communicate my expectations clearly to my team so they are understood						
I check for understanding from team members						
I give clear, motivating and constructive feedback to help others achieve success						
I share the organisation's vision & mission in an inspirational way so people understand where we are headed and the opportunities the vision/mission will bring						
I provide feedback and evaluation to individuals and/or collective team performance and I am confident doing so						
People know where I stand on a matter						

TEAM BUILDING:	Almost Never	Rarely	Sometimes	Often	Almost Always	N/A
I actively take an interest in my team members and know about issues impacting their lives						
I acknowledge and praise my team for work well done						
I treat team members with appreciation, dignity and compassion						
Once expectations are understood, I empower my team to take action						
I generally understand how team members feel about their co-workers						
I promote teamwork i.e. encouraging open communication and working together to achieve given goals						

I recognise and utilise the talents of others (this may be my own team or people outside it)						
I proactively support the development of individuals on my team						
I release resources (financial and human) to support the development of my team						
I create an environment where individuals stretch themselves and achieve more than they believed was possible						
Along with team members, I have a track record for achieving the goals and objectives we have set						

ETHICS:	Almost Never	Rarely	Sometimes	Often	Almost Always	N/A
Even under pressure I follow ethical/ biblical standards that will not be compromised						
I honour promises and commitments						
I admit to my mistakes						
I engage in regular self-reflection to assess my outcomes and improvements needed						

LEADERSHIP:	Almost Never	Rarely	Sometimes	Often	Almost Always	N/A
I am consistent in the way I treat anyone. No one person is treated differently from another.						
I am intellectually curious. i.e. I want to learn all the time						
I understand the organisation's direction, vision mission values and strategy						
I work constructively under stress and pressure – I do not bury my head under the sand!						
I create an environment where team and customer satisfaction is expected and focused upon						

I demonstrate an appropriate level of patience						
I create an atmosphere of drive, excitement and personal investment						
I manage my time effectively						
I confront problems head-on and work to resolve them immediately						
I ask others for feedback to enhance performance (mine and the team)						
I act on feedback appropriately without seeing it as personal or beneath me						
I listen well so that I can understand what the other person or people are communicating						

without interrupting						
I create an environment of trust, safety and appropriate risk-taking						
I actively assess the strengths and skills of my team members so they can be fully utilised so they feel empowered						
I am actively seeking leader/s I can nurture to succeed me in order to ensure the mission continues beyond me						

SUPPORT:	Almost Never	Rarely	Sometimes	Often	Almost Always	N/A
I have an active network of professional relationships with other ministers or those who are expert in their filed, inside and outside the church						
I regularly have a mentoring or coaching session with someone who has more experience and insight than me						

My areas of strengths are:

In order to be a more effective leader, I will need to address the following areas:

I will take the following action to address the issues above:

ACTION 1	Date to be completed:
ACTION 2	Date to be completed:
ACTION 3	Date to be completed:

For more information and support visit growthechurchnow.com

NOTES

www.ingramcontent.com/pod-product-compliance
Lightning Source LLC
Chambersburg PA
CBHW081413070526
44583CB00020B/2784

9781999839772